Ranka —

May your Speaking Career reach great heights!

Thanks
Paul Tritton
Nov 15/09,
Vancouver, BC

Order this book online at www.trafford.com/07-1597
or email orders@trafford.com

Most Trafford titles are also available at major online book retailers.

© Copyright 2008 Paul Talbot.

All rights reserved. No part of this publication may be reproduced, stored in a retrieval system, or transmitted, in any form or by any means, electronic, mechanical, photocopying, recording, or otherwise, without the written prior permission of the author.

Illustrated by: Ian Skelly
Edited by: André Tassé
Cover Design/Artwork by: Paul Talbot
Designed by: Pender Copy

Note for Librarians: A cataloguing record for this book is available from Library and Archives Canada at www.collectionscanada.ca/amicus/index-e.html

Printed in Victoria, BC, Canada.

ISBN: 978-1-4251-3949-0

We at Trafford believe that it is the responsibility of us all, as both individuals and corporations, to make choices that are environmentally and socially sound. You, in turn, are supporting this responsible conduct each time you purchase a Trafford book, or make use of our publishing services. To find out how you are helping, please visit www.trafford.com/responsiblepublishing.html

Our mission is to efficiently provide the world's finest, most comprehensive book publishing service, enabling every author to experience success. To find out how to publish your book, your way, and have it available worldwide, visit us online at www.trafford.com/10510

Trafford
PUBLISHING

www.trafford.com

North America & international
toll-free: 1 888 232 4444 (USA & Canada)
phone: 250 383 6864 ♦ fax: 250 383 6804
email: info@trafford.com

The United Kingdom & Europe
phone: +44 (0)1865 722 113 ♦ local rate: 0845 230 9601
facsimile: +44 (0)1865 722 868 ♦ email: info.uk@trafford.com

10 9 8 7 6 5 4 3 2 1

HOW TO EARN MONEY AS A SPEAKER©

INTRODUCTION

Dear Friend and Fellow Speaker:

This amazing book is written for YOU with the hope that it will help you boost your career and earn a lucrative income in the business of being a Professional Speaker.

I created and founded the "Clutter" series which includes the following:

- "Clear the Clutter and Simplify Your Life©"

- "Clear the Clutter for Seniors©"

- "Simple and Forgotten Things – Voluntary Simplicity©"

- "How to be a Full/Part-Time Clutter Organizer©"

All of the above are available as separate workshops and each one has a workbook / manual to assist not only the facilitator but the participants. I have also written and produced:

- "Be a Winner - Steps to Success©": a motivational, goal-setting booklet with audio

CD that will help you find clarity as well as focus on your dreams, desires and goals in life.

- And the following booklets:

    - "Setting Goals for Cleaning Your Clutter!©"

    - "Change One Thing©"

    - "Will Your Christmas Be Cluttered©"

    - "Simple and Forgotten Things - Voluntary Simplicity©"

To obtain more information on my workshops and services, please visit my website:

www.dialaspeaker.com

So, as Creator of the "Clutter" series and co-founder of END THE CLUTTER INTERNATIONAL, I am happy to share with you my "secrets", hence helping you become the very best that you can be. If you will combine the information in this book with your present knowledge, experience and PASSION, you will have some dynamic tools for increasing your productivity and revenue.

Included in this book is a special bonus, my gift to you, titled "How to Facilitate with Facts, Feelings and Fun!©" and its companion "Handbook":

THE HANDBOOK© is in addition to the book "How to Facilitate With Facts, Feeling and Fun©" and forms part of the complete package that you would receive in my one or two day workshops of the same name. It is a practical how-to book on facilitating your own workshop or seminar.

As a speaker / trainer, only YOU know if you are the expert in your given field. Like all of us, you have had to pay your dues by offering FREE workshops. Now the time has come to move forward and START CHARGING for your services.

I hope that the workshop and printed manuals will give you the opportunity to explore further your talents, skills, knowledge and passion; and my words to you are...

GO FOR IT!

I hope that this section of the book will give you new ideas, suggestions and ways in which you can facilitate your workshops or seminars. On a personal basis, I would be happy to coach you individually. Please call me direct for details.

Finally, I sincerely wish you the best possible future as a speaker and may all your dreams come true.

Kind personal regards,

Paul Talbot
International Speaker / Trainer,
Simplicity Coach, Clutter Therapist, Author
Creator/Founder and Trainer of the "Clutter" Series
Founding Member of End The Clutter
International

How to Earn Money as a Speaker©
ISBN 1 870048 01 6
Copyright 1986-2007
Revised, updated and expanded
Thanks to Len Comaniuk and André Tassé for revising and updating this book
Illustrations / Cartoons by Ian Skelly

How to Facilitate with Facts, Feelings, and Fun©
Revised update 2007; Thanks to André Tassé
Copyright 2002 – 2007
By Paul Talbot, Vancouver, B.C. Canada

ACKNOWLEDGEMENTS

Taking the time and energy to write and produce these books would not have happened without the encouragement of so many wonderful people in my life.

1998, I underwent surgery for cancer and spent a good part of 1999 in recovery. This truly resulted in me making a great many changes in my life such as: *"How and where could I generate an income on which to live?"*. So many changes took place such as relationships and friendships in these areas due to my health, low energy, and having to put myself FIRST. My values in life changed and my family became my inspiration.

Sadly, my Mum passed away very suddenly on November 2, 1999. I thank her for her love and encouragement and truly feel my recovery was as a result of her, and all the love and support I received from family and friends.

I dedicate this manual to the following persons:

- Special thanks to my late parents for their love and specialness, to my brothers and sisters for the love and joy we share. In particular to my sister Wendy, here in Vancouver, for just being there and supporting me. "You're the best!";

- To Ed Bailey – for originally word processing all the manuals and putting up with me changing my mind countless times, and for his suggestions and creativity;

- To Linda Shaw – for believing in me and being there;

- To Marie Tomko – for always encouraging me;

- To Sandra and David Craig – for inspiring me and pushing me on;

- To Michael New, Glen Cropsey (you will always be greatly missed), Dorothy Blandford, Vee Maurio, Aleta Brown and Barb Davies.

- Thanks to André Tassé, Harlene Cloutier and Len Comaniuk for all your word processing and computer help. Without each of you this book would not happened.

- To the wonderful staff and friends at St. Paul's Hospital in Vancouver for helping me during my personal experience with cancer, during and after my recovery, thank you.

- To my friends worldwide for being my friends and supporting me, for believing in me and helping me through some difficult times in my life;

- To the thousands of people who allowed me, as a speaker, to talk, share, laugh, and sometimes cry (with joy), THANK YOU. May your life as a speaker be one of joy, love and much laughter; and, finally,

- ❏ To the Universe – for letting me be "me" and allowing me to continue my journey on this earth with great love, joy and happiness, to share my skills, knowledge, experiences and life with you.

Thank you

TABLE OF CONTENTS

HOW TO EARN MONEY AS A SPEAKER© 1
  Introduction 1
  Acknowledgements 5
  How to Earn Money as a Speaker 11
  Who Hires Speakers 11
  How Much Money Can You Make as a
    Speaker 13
  Setting Your Fee 15
  How to Become F-a-m-o-u-s!!! 19
  Learning to Speak 24
    Toastmasters International (24); National
    Speakers Association (25); 25 Steps to
    Speaking With Confidence (26); Overview
    of the Quality of Speakers and Speeches
    (29)
  Testing Before Investing 29
  Your Program 30
    Putting Together Your Program: Public or In-
    house (30); What to Call Your Program (31);
    Who are you? (31); Choosing the Topic
    (32); Developing an Effective Program (33);
    Program Materials (33); Program
    Registration (34); The Best Days of The
    Week to Hold a Seminar / Workshop Are:
    (35); Factors Involved in Scheduling Your
    Program (35)
  Advertising 36
    The one-step promotion cycle (37); The
    two-step promotional cycle. (37); Making
    up Your "Press Kit" (40); Preparing Your
    Brochure (42); Preparing Your "Demo" Tape
    (45); Newsletters (46); Using Other People

to Market You (47); Referrals (49); Using Sponsors (50)

Know Your Audience 51
Preparing Your Introduction And Closing (52); Answering Questions (52); Awarding Certificates (53); How to Handle a Dissatisfied Participant (53)

Tape Recording Your Presentation 53
The Venue 54
Selecting And Renting Meeting Rooms (54); Seating Arrangements (55); Audio Visual (55); Serving Coffee (55); In-house Meals (55)

Paying Your Bill 56
Publishing And Marketing Your Own Products
.... 56
The Monograph (56); Your First Book (57); Tape Cassettes or CD's (57); Selling Your Products (58)

The First Year as a Professional Speaker 61
Sample Speaking Agreement 65
Just a Few Questions (67)

HOW TO FACILITATE WITH FACTS, FEELINGS AND FUN© 69
Six Ways to Make this Course More Valuable
.... 70
Sources of Speaker Income 72
Preparation Saves the Day 73
Preparation Checklist (74); Equipment (74)

Let the Show Begin 76
Welcome (76); Background of The Facilitator (76); House Keeping Information (77); Ground Rules (77); Tailoring Your Agenda (78)

Monitor Yourself 79

    Watch the Participants (80); Feedback (82); Pace Yourself (82); Keeping Them Interested (83); Conducting a One Day Workshop (84); Conducting On-going Evening Sessions (84); Educate, Inform and Entertain (85)
  Closing 86
    Evaluation Forms (87)
  Exceptions 88
    Lateness and Absenteeism (88); Disruptions (88)

THE HANDBOOK© 90
  Free give-away(s) 97
  Speaker products 98

Handouts 101
  About the Author 103
    Background / Experience: (103); Accomplishments: (104); Mission Statement: (105); Vision: (105); Commitment: (105)
  Course Evaluation 107
  Comments from Participants of Paul Talbot's "Clear the Clutter and Simplicity Workshops" 109
  Services Offered by Paul Talbot 114
  Famous Quotes 118

NOTES

How to Earn Money as a Speaker

Your success in the speaking and seminar business will be determined more by your ability to market and promote yourself than by your program content or presentation. A good program and an effective presentation are not sufficient for success in this business.

This book is designed to help you MARKET and PROMOTE yourself as a Professional Speaker.

You will not become a successful speaker overnight. It takes time, commitment, and that unpopular word "work".

Who Hires Speakers

There are two basic ways speakers are hired. The first is to be engaged by a business, group or organization which generally pays a SET FEE on the length of the speech, seminar or workshop presented by the speaker. The second method is to be paid on a per person basis which is calculated by the number of people present in the audience rather than a set fee determined in advance.

Some of the organizations you may wish to contact are:

- Business & Trade Organizations
- Convention Planners
- Business Firms & Corporations
- Professional Associations
- Civic Groups
- Fraternal Organizations
- Service Organizations
- Political Affiliations
- Athletics Clubs
- Church Groups

Of course, the types of organizations you choose will be tailored to your own program content and presentation.

Scan the yellow pages of the phone book or the

NOTES

various reference sources available at the public library.

Another method is to PROMOTE YOUR OWN speeches, seminars, and / or workshops to the general public in a variety of ways. However, you may choose to use BOTH methods and I'll discuss this later on in the book.

How Much Money Can You Make as a Speaker

If you are promoting your own program(s) to the general public, your income will be determined by how skilled you are in marketing yourself. Once again, I cannot over-emphasize this fact... regardless of the quality of your presentation, it does you absolutely no good whatsoever if you are speaking to an EMPTY ROOM.

Your very first payday as a PUBLIC SPEAKER is most significant; you are now a PROFESSIONAL. From that day forward your fees will continue to rise slowly or they will soar depending upon your ability to MARKET YOURSELF.

The highest paid speakers are celebrities. Johnny Carson receives

NOTES

$40,000.00 and Henry Kissinger $35,000.00 for each speech they give! Most speakers receive CONSIDERABLY LESS. It is not unusual to earn $100,000 to $500,000 per year as a PROFESSIONAL SPEAKER.

Make no mistake about it, professional speakers are among the HIGHEST paid people in the world. A Professional speaker can charge the following fees:

Half day speech . . . . $ 500 *plus*

For an out of area speech where there is travel involved (all your expenses to be paid)

. . . . $ 2,000 *plus*

Full Day (depending upon topic and event)

. . . . $ 2,000 *plus*

Check Yellow Pages for "Public Speakers", call to find out what they are paying, depending upon topic, area and country. Remember also to charge for your EXPENSES.

Note: For out of town presentations, I always ask for a prepaid return ticket.

NOTES

SETTING YOUR FEE

When you receive a call from a prospective client, do not say immediately you are available. Never, never say "yes" to a booking without asking some important questions.

Find out if you are going to be working with a large, medium, or small audience. The size of the audience has much to do with what you will earn. Not only how much, but in what manner or from what sources. You can charge a flat fee, a per person basis or a 50-50 split of the fees AFTER expenses.

How long of a speech or program did you have in mind? You want to learn whether it is a one hour speech, a half day seminar or a full day program.

Check around and find out what others are charging. People are cost-conscious, therefore by setting your fee a little lower you may attract the work. You may decide to vary your fee depending upon the length of each program, i.e. three hour program vs. full day etc.

Are you interested in publicizing this event?

NOTES

If he/she says "yes", say "*I can come in a day early and do some publicity for you and your organization if you can set up some radio and TV interviews*". Also stress you are available for newspaper interviews.
Don't miss this change to PROMOTE.

"*As long as I am coming in earlier, would you like me to do a special program for your key people?*" If he/she says "yes" you can arrange an additional fee for this.

"*In what way would you like to use my educational materials?*"

State that you have some excellent material through your books and tape cassettes. Either have a table at the back of the room (near the doorway as they go OUT) and display your materials, or ask if they wish a package to be INCLUDED for everyone in the fee.

Ask, "*Which way would work best for you?*"

Use the direct approach, you have materials you WANT to sell them.

This is an extremely important question ... "*Who did you have last year?*" You will soon become familiar with your colleagues and therefore will have an idea as to their topic and fee.

"*What is the budget for this year's program?*"

NOTES

When this is revealed you may learn that they have a budget for more than you were willing to charge them. You certainly want to take advantage of all available income ... you are worth it!

On the other hand they may have a budget that is LESS than your normal fee. If they do not have enough money to pay your normal fee there are two things you can do.

First, it can help them by finding a way they can make money with you in order to afford your fees. Think of ways you can help them pay your fee by raising money as a result of YOU BEING THERE.

The second is you may wish to LOWER your fee. This can be especially beneficial to you if it is a large nationwide organization. The whole idea is to get as much work as you can while you are there.

There are other factors involved in setting your fees, such as, how many people will be there. Sometimes your fee is set on a per person basis. Decide on your minimum fee, check and find out what others are charging. More money comes with one thing, and this is something you must decide yourself if you are going to make it BIG in the speaking and seminar business. YOU MUST BECOME FAMOUS. The more

NOTES

NOTES

famous you are, the more money you will be paid for doing the same speech or seminar. If you don't work on becoming famous, you will only be able to command the minimum fee. On top of that, you probably won't have much work because the general public will be unfamiliar with who you are and what you do.

Making yourself FAMOUS is something you have to work on EVERY DAY if you want to build a LUCRATIVE paid speaking business. Starting now it must be part of your PERSONAL GOAL PLANNING.

If you are a professional speaker with a quality program and an effective presentation, you have two choices:

A. You can remain low-profile sharing your wonderful message with various organizations for a minimal fee, or...

B. You can work towards celebrity status (within various frames of reference) and share EXACTLY the SAME message for BIG BUCKS.

SO LET'S GET F-A-M-O-U-S!!!

How to Become F-A-M-O-U-S!!!

NOTES

The FASTEST way to build your name and become FAMOUS is to get published. Perhaps you are conjuring up images of novelists who send manuscripts to dozens of book publishers each week and consider themselves fortunate IF they receive a rejection. Book publishers receive far more manuscripts than you or I can begin to imagine. Most of these manuscripts NEVER get read, let alone published.

With editors of MAGAZINES, however, it is an entirely different story. They are CONSTANTLY looking for NEW material and are most eager for contributors from talented, fresh sources. Bear in mind that they must have NEW material to fill their periodical month after month or better yet, week after week.

Be honest with yourself. Haven't you at

NOTES

least at one time or another read a magazine article and though to yourself, "I could write something which would be of far greater interest to the readers of this periodical?" And in all probability you are correct, and yet what is the basic difference between you and the person who wrote that article? That person took ACTION.

You must write articles that your potential clients will read in TRADE MAGAZINES. Getting published is a numbers game. Don't give up, keep on mailing them out.

Check with the Public Library that lists all Associations and Newspapers, magazines, trade publications etc. Find out the name of the editor, and if possible, contact that person by phone. Tell him/her that you have written an article that would be of interest to their readers. Have the title of the article in mind so that you can give it to him/her if he/she asks. In other words, <u>be prepared</u>.

Many of the magazines will also pay you a fee so in fact they are paying you for the privilege of advertising YOUR BUSINESS.

You can write ONE article and change the title and some of the content so that it can be submitted to several publications. Remember, the more articles you submit, the greater the chances will be of having your article published.

When submitting your article to the various publications, NEVER under any circumstances do so without including YOUR picture. People respond well to visuals and you want them to be able to correlate what you have written with your appearance. Studies have proven that they will be more likely to remember you if they have seen your picture with the article. In fact, it is an excellent idea to put your picture on everything that has your name on it such as your business cards and stationery. The name of the game is "Don't forget me."

When you do get your articles published, make copies of them because you will need them for your press kit. This will help you to become famous.

The speakers who will become well known are the speakers who are DIFFERENT. Your program can be very similar in content to that of other speakers, however, you must find a way to distinguish YOURSELF from the thousands of other individuals

NOTES

who call themselves Professional Speakers. There is nothing worse in this business than to hear someone in charge of hiring a speaker say "*There is no sense in having Mr. ...., he's just like Mr. .... and we heard him two months ago.*"

Don't be like ANYBODY ELSE, be different and be <u>YOURSELF</u>. Observe other Speakers, attend their presentations and study exactly what it is in the material and delivery that causes you to remember some and not others. Learn to be different, novel, innovative.

Never ignore any situation where you might get your name known. Talk to people in public places, pass out your business cards, and CONSTANTLY PROMOTE YOURSELF. Notice I said <u>YOURSELF</u>.

It is imperative that you promote <u>YOURSELF</u> rather than your program. We are certainly not ignoring the value of what you have to say but it will never get said if You cannot get in front of an audience. The public wants IMAGE. They must become interested in YOU before they become interested in your program.

Why do you think the multi-million dollar corporations use big name celebrities to endorse everything from automobiles to yogurt? IDENTIFICATION.

NOTES

NOTES

The public must be able to identify with you as a person. Become FAMOUS, achieve celebrity status, and the public will pay big money to hear what you couldn't give away free before.

Starting from absolute obscurity, as I well know, can be more than a little discouraging. To use another cliché, but one that is true, "*The first step is the hardest.*" The more you do to become known, the more others will do for you. Promoting yourself is one thing but having others do it for you simply because they have benefited from your program is the best possible advertising you can get.

As each day goes by on your journey to fame and fortune, you will find that you will have to reach out less, and that people will be coming to YOU more and more. But don't forget, at first YOU must do all the reaching.

Whenever you are going to give a speech or seminar, publicize it as much as possible. If you are different, interesting and informative, the radio, TV and newspapers will be more than willing, in fact in some cases eager, to interview you.

Think about the talk shows and / or open line shows in your area.

Remember, "*if you don't ASK you don't GET*" and follow these essential points in order to achieve celebrity status as a PROFESSIONAL SPEAKER.

- Have your articles published. ✓
- Always consent to interviews. ✓
- Appear on as many talk, open line shows as possible. ✓
- Include your photo whenever you can. ✓
- Promote yourself everywhere you can. ✓
- BE DIFFERENT. ✓

If you follow these SIX suggestions on a day-to-day basis, you will soon be on your way to fame, and shortly thereafter to fortune as well.

LEARNING TO SPEAK

Toastmasters International

An organization totally dedicated to personal growth and communication excellence is TOASTMASTERS INTERNATIONAL. The club was formed in

NOTES

1942 *"to afford practice and training in the art of public speaking and in presiding over meetings, and to promote sociability and good fellowship among its members."*

Most Toastmaster clubs meet weekly and there are breakfast, lunch, dinner and evening meetings to accommodate a variety of situations. Toastmasters is a suitable organization for the novice speaker, the veteran, or anyone in between. It is an excellent way to perfect your craft in a POSITIVE and relaxed atmosphere.

National Speakers Association

NSA does not book speakers but provides training and resource materials for the professional speaker. By joining NSA you will have an opportunity to meet other famous and less famous speakers, hear them speak, and share ideas with them.

National Speakers
Association
1500 South Priest Drive
Tempe, Arizona 85281
Tel: (480) 968-2552
Fax: (480) 968-0911

Check out and see if there is a chapter in your area.

NOTES

25 Steps to Speaking With Confidence

NOTES

1) Prepare in advance.

2) Identify the reason(s) for speaking and what you hope the results will be.

3) Find out as much as you can about the audience.

4) Don't try and write your talk in one sitting - jot down ideas as they come along.

5) Use simple, short sentences ... K I S.

6) Choose two or three points and illustrate them with examples.

7) Keep a file of amusing stories; try to personalize them.

8) Steer clear of jargon, abbreviations and statistics if possible.

9) Be precise and avoid clichés.

10) Write points on cards but don't read as a script.

11) Rehearse aloud several times because familiarity breeds confidence.

12) An interesting voice has a variety of pitch (highs and lows), volume and speed, including silent pauses.

13) Practice reading aloud to young children or into a tape recorder.

14) Remember... nerves often make you speak high and fast, so practice low and slow.

15) Imagine your voice is a laser beam and try to penetrate the wall into the next room.

16) Repeat "Hong Kong, Ding Dong" several times a day to develop a deeper and more resonant voice.

17) Wear comfortable shoes - squashed toes show on your face.

18) Empty your pockets of lose change; don't wear distracting jewelry.

19) Don't dwell on failure; concentrate on visualizing a positive outcome.

20) Be enthusiastic!

21) Walk slowly to the speaking spot, look at the audience, SMILE, and take a couple of deep breaths before you begin.

NOTES

22) Try and include EVERYBODY in your eye contact.

23) Your expression should be happy.

24) Make appropriate gestures and avoid clutching the lectern with white knuckles or fiddling with pens, paper clips, etc.

25) Adrenalin and alcohol don't mix - have one when you have finished. You deserve it!

          Good luck!

NOTES

Overview of the Quality of Speakers and Speeches

This survey by Lilly Walters was taken in 2000 in the United States. Results may vary depending upon topic, speaker and how personal the presentation may apply to the respondents.

Audience members recall and clarity...

Message	37%
Real Life	21%
Style and Eloquence	14%
Passion	9%
Humour and Heart	6%
Compassion	5%
Connect	5%
Stories	4%

TESTING BEFORE INVESTING

Test marketing can help you to determine what the public demand will be for your program and what changes you will need to make to market it.

A test run on a local basis can be accomplished on a budget for about $500-600. (£200 up)

The two most difficult obstacles that you will have to overcome in the speaking and seminar business are:

- Targeting your audience.

- Promoting and marketing your services.

Your Program

Putting Together Your Program: Public or In-house

There are two ways to present your program:

The first way is to have the people come to you. Your advertising, marketing and promotion would be targeted to a certain segment of the general public that would have potential interest in your subject matter.

The second way is for you to go to your audience. This would be in-house. The organization you are working for would set up and provide an audience, accommodation, etc. You would know

NOTES

in advance what to expect as far as your compensation is concerned.

The in-house seminar provides financial security. However, the public seminar can provide a much larger income but greater risks.

What to Call Your Program

Your ability to market and promote yourself will be strongly influenced by what you decide to call your program. A successful program title should consist of the following elements:

Who are you?

If possible your name should be part of the title of your program. The purpose of this is not ego, but association. You want your participants to associate you with your subject matter. It is much easier to sell a program when it is attached to a personality than one that just states the subject matter. Linking your name to the program helps the participants to realize there is a real person behind the program.

I have noticed that Dale Carnegie uses their name in some of their programs, i.e. The Dale Carnegie Sales Training Program, the Dale Carnegie Management Program etc.

NOTES

Choosing the Topic

NOTES

Your title should correspond as closely as possible to your subject matter. If you are presenting a success training seminar, you should state that in your title. Don't call it something else just to be clever.

You can increase your chances for SUCCESS if you choose a subject that PERSONALLY INTERESTS YOU. The more you are committed to your topic the greater your chance of success will be as a professional speaker.

There are some additional considerations that must be addressed in choosing your topic. They are:

1) Is there a long-term demand for your topic? Will people still be interested in your subject matter 5-7 years from now? Stay away from subjects that are fads or have limited appeal.

2) Are people willing to PAY for the information you have to offer on this topic?

If you can show a person that they can make money or become more successful in their occupation they will consider your presentation a cost effective investment worth paying for.

Usually people are willing to pay for training out of their own pocket if they are self-employed. If they have an employer, they expect their employer to pay for it.

Developing an Effective Program

There are several things you do to develop an effective seminar, workshop or training program.

- Make sure your material is interesting, informative and useful.

- Don't waste their time.

- Be entertaining as well as informative.

- Get your audience involved.

- Make your audience as comfortable as possible.

Program Materials

When ever you are going to present a seminar, a speech or another presentation, have your books, tapes, etc. shipped several weeks prior to your speaking engagement.

I have found best to take with me handout materials. In some cases you may wish to forward an original and let your client reproduce all handouts. A

NOTES

word of warning: telephone ahead to make sure that original was received (this did happen to me, mine got lost in the mail!)

Program Registration

It is essential that you have competent help at the registration table if you are presenting a seminar or workshop. In most cases it would be wise to hire temporary help for the half day or day. You want to project a PROFESSIONAL IMAGE.

Miscellaneous reminders for a SUCCESSFUL seminar / workshop:

- Check and recheck your hotel meeting and sleeping rooms reservations.

- Have extra copies of your presentation materials. (See my comment in previous section).

- Repeat all the participants' questions before answering them.

- Keep on schedule.

- Maintain eye contact with your audience.

- Acknowledge all phone and mail registrants.

NOTES

- Use name tags.

- Make it easy for your participants to find you.

- Have coffee, water or refreshments.

The Best Days of The Week to Hold a Seminar / Workshop Are:

According to a survey done in the United States by organizations that hire speakers, it was found that the days ranked in the following order, from most to least convenient to employees and their organisation:

1. Thursday   2. Wednesday

3. Tuesday   4. Friday

5. Saturday   6. Monday

7. Sunday

Factors Involved in Scheduling Your Program

- Vacation periods.
- National or Religious holidays.
- Major local or national events.
- Competition.
- Public transportation.

NOTES

- Daylight savings time.
- Hotel bookings.
- Labour strikes or pending strikes.

NOTES

ADVERTISING

The speaking and seminar business is a PROMOTIONAL sensitive business. Your success will be determined by developing a marketing plan that can be tested and modified inexpensively.

Remember, two-thirds of your acquisition costs will be for MARKETING. This includes promotional designs, copyrighting, telephone marketing, web-site development and maintenance, media costs, mailing expenses, advertising etc.

Focus on your MARKET from the beginning. The key, find a group of people (your market) which you can reach at a reasonable cost.

The two best methods to promote your seminar or workshop are:

The one-step promotion cycle

This type of promotion is usually used in securing a contract with a captive or in-house audience. Basically you convince your client through your promotional material to hire you to present your program to a captive audience. You sell them on the idea that your presentation will produce a SPECIFIC BENEFIT or SOLVE a particular problem facing the organization, enabling them to be more efficient or make more money in their respective field.

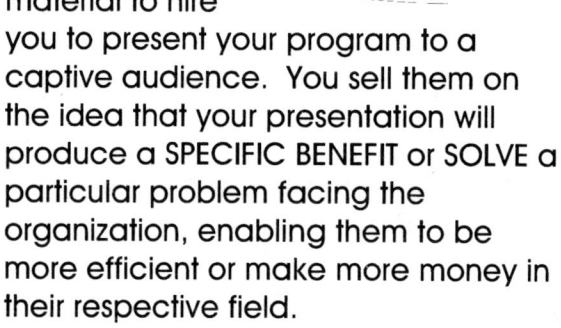

The two-step promotional cycle.

This is frequently used in investment, real estate and expensive self-employment seminars. Basically it works this way: the public is invited to a FREE LECTURE on a particular subject. While the FREE LECTURE is generally informative, the main purpose is to SELL the prospective participant(s) on future seminar(s), workshop(s), or training

NOTES

programs(s) which will be given for an ADDITIONAL specified fee. The fee can range from $25.00 to $1,000 (£10.00 and up).

The success or failure of the two-step has a great deal to do with the presenter's personality and ability to win over his audience.

Newspapers and magazines can be one of the most cost effective way you can promote your seminars and workshops (due to the number of people it will reach).

Check out:

- ✓ Advertising rates and charges
- ✓ Circulation
- ✓ Editorial Profile
- ✓ Representatives and their branch offices
- ✓ Deadline for copy submission
- ✓ Ad sizes and column widths

NOTES

You can rent or purchase mailing lists: check them out and inquire about:

NOTES

- ✓ Sources of the list: Name of the magazine, company, association or group that the list was obtained from.

- ✓ Rental rates, per hundred, per thousand, the minimum number you can rent.

- ✓ Any other charges.

- ✓ How the labels are addressed.

- ✓ Update frequency.

Generally the return rate for DIRECT MAIL is from 1% to 5% of the ENTIRE MAILING. Test marketing for direct mail is about 3 to 4,000 pieces.

A properly prepared display ad can mean the difference between an ad that pulls and one that gets little or no attention.

One of the best ways to design ads is to look at similar ones. Check the business sections to find out what other seminar speakers are presenting.

Depending upon who your audience will be, it will be necessary for you to place your ad in:

- Main section or Main News
- Current or Lifestyle
- Sports Section
- Economy or Business Section

The best months of the year to promote seminars and workshops are as follows:

September

   January

      April

         March

            February

               October

                  May

                     June

                        December

                           August

                             July

Making up Your "Press Kit"

A press kit is similar to a model's portfolio.

Your press kit will be your prospect's first introduction to you, so every item in it

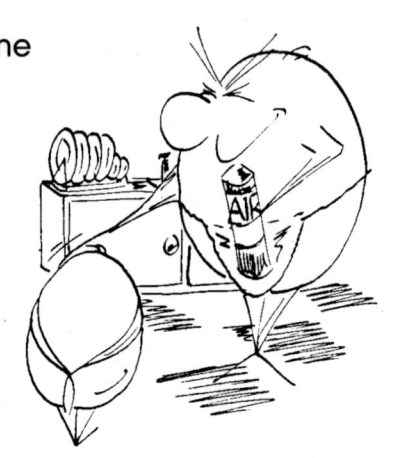

NOTES

should sell you. It should create the image you want your prospect to have of you. When you make up your press kit keep this word foremost in your mind: QUALITY. You must look SUCCESSFUL. No one want to hire a person who is struggling to get to the top. It must look like you're already there! The feeling you want to create is that you are an EXPERIENCED, ACCOMPLISHED, COMPETENT, and SUCCESSFUL SPEAKER.

You may be nervously anticipating your first payday as a public speaker or you may have some limited experience. In either case, the recipient of your press kit must believe that you are already a successful speaker. Everything in your kit should reinforce this idea.

With each speaking engagement you can change your press kit, building and adding more information about your experience, and proficiency as a speaker.

NOTES

Your press kit should include the following:

- Letters of recommendation – these are letters from companies, groups and associations that have worked with you.

- A biography. Have a written biography of your education, business background, and your accomplishments.

- A copy of your book(s), CD's and/or Video DVD's if you have one. The best way to get a speaking engagement is to send a copy of your book.

- A sample brochure. Include your best quality brochure. This will help sell you to those in charge of hiring and ultimately to the participants at the seminar who will RECOMMEND you to their friends.

I have prepared a section in this manual on the do's and don't's of an effective brochure, such as design, graphics, paper quality, typesetting etc. Read it carefully.

Preparing Your Brochure

Most organizations receive 60 to 100 pieces of direct mail each week, most of them are just thrown away.

NOTES

NOTES

Therefore, you must get the recipient to OPEN your envelope or folder.

The most effective brochure is one that sells BENEFITS. What will they gain from your speaking services or seminar. Your message must be clear, concise, comprehensive in ONE reading. A good photograph of yourself will help assure the reader that you are a real special person!

Shop around, check out the prices, quality of the work of graphic artists, typesetters, etc. Can you do it all at one place or must you involve more than one company? What do you save, time, money or... ?

The size and colour of your brochure is important. Try to keep it to a standard size format, it can be folded in numerous ways to change its appearance and appeal. Different coloured inks and coloured papers will add an appearance of quality to your brochure.

Many brochures use testimonials. Sometimes they can work for you by adding to your credibility because the reader has never heard of you before.

Your brochure and advertising should contain the following information

- Benefits.
- Costs.
- Registration or sign-up procedure.
- Payment.
- Where can the prospective clients reach you?
- Background information on YOU!
- What materials are included in your program?
- What options does the participant have if he cannot attend this seminar?
- How can he reply?
- An Act-Now-Motivation (free gift, early-bird discount).
- Testimonials.
- Tax Deductible Savings.
- Money back guarantee or Refund Policy.

NOTES

Preparing Your "Demo" Tape

A demo tape is simply a SHORT cassette recording that can be given to prospective clients so that they can hear a portion of your live presentation. Remember, you are in the business of "speaking" not "writing", potential clients WANT TO HEAR YOUR VOICE. In reality, this should be an audition tape, for this is what it is.

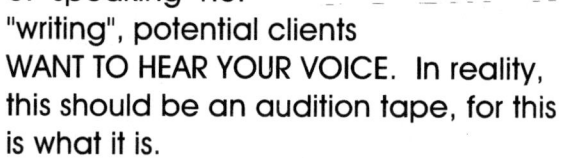

A demo tape should be longer than 15 minutes in length. This is a sufficient amount of time for someone to get the general 'feeling' of what you sound like and what kind of material you are presenting.

You want to show your prospective client that you can INSPIRE, EDUCATE AND MOTIVATE your audience. You want them to feel that you could have the same effect if you work with their organization. I urge you to be particularly aware of the entertainment factor. Everyone wants to laugh (in spite of all surveys in the world!)

NOTES

Your demo tape will be more effective if you have someone introduce you on the tape. The announcer's message should last no more than one minute at the beginning of the tape and one minute at the end.

You will need a recording studio to work with you on this so that your original tapes can be cut and edited. Make sure that your tape is FIRST CLASS. A demo tape is part of your self-promotion and is well worth the effort. Remember, your demo tape is your best salesman.

Newsletters

A newsletter is one of the finest marketing tools a speaker can use. It's an excellent way of picking up referral business.

Some possible items to include in your newsletter are:

- A schedule of where you are speaking.

- Reviews of books and cassette packages.

- Articles and information closely related to your program.

NOTES

NOTES

A newsletter is also an excellent way to market your products through mail order.

It is not necessary to publish a newsletter every month. A high quality newsletter 3 or 4 times a year will produce good results. Remember, your newsletter will project your image, therefore use good quality paper – you want to look SUCCESSFUL.

Newsletters can be time consuming to produce. Give some thought as to the length, number of pages, frequency etc. BEFORE you start going into production.

Will it be free (by request only) or will you charge for it?

Using Other People to Market You

Most speakers book their own seminars. Others use booking agencies. Booking agencies or speakers bureaus as they are called, work with numerous speakers. They receive calls form meeting planners, associations, corporations and business's that are looking for specific types of speakers.

NOTES

The booking agent then matches the speaker with the type of presentation requested by the organization.

For securing the contract, the booking agent receives a percentage of the speaker's fee; this is usually 25% to 35%. Some booking agents may want a percentage of your tape and book sales as well, but this is negotiable.

Remember, there will be a fee, which you pay, to the booking agent or speakers bureau. Although there is no guarantee that this will result in paid engagements, your name, photograph, topics etc. will appear in their directory which they will mail out to organizations and companies that use their services.

Booking agents are usually looking for speakers that command high fees – the reason is simple: they receive at least 25% of YOUR fee. They are not going to do all the work for you. All a booking agent can do is open doors for you. It's up to you to carry the ball from there.

You may wish to consider hiring your own booking agent who works for you exclusively. This person would be part of your staff and is usually paid an hourly wage plus a bonus for securing your booking and they work EXCLUSIVELY for you.

The following persons / organizations can be helpful to you and your staff:

Prime Performers
The Studio
5 Kinderpore Avenue
LONDON NW3 7SX

World Convention Dates
79 Washington Street
Hampstead, NY 11550

Walters Speakers Bureau
Royal Publishing
PO Box 398
Glendora, CA 91740
Tel: (626) 335-8069
Fax: (626) 335-6125

<u>Note:</u>   Walter's newsletter "Sharing Ideas" is great. Subscribe by e-mail on www.speakandgrowrich.com

As you can see, the name of the game in the speaking business is BOOKINGS!

Keep in mind that the convention planners do not work FOR YOU. So you must work WITH THEM.

Referrals

A job well done for one division of a company provides you with the perfect opportunity to get referrals to OTHER divisions.

NOTES

☞ **Ask ...**

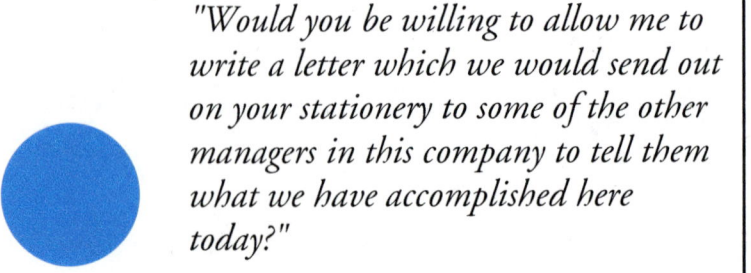

"Would you be willing to allow me to write a letter which we would send out on your stationery to some of the other managers in this company to tell them what we have accomplished here today?"

You must ASK for this letter.

If you give a good presentation you will generally find them willing to write the letter for two reasons:

- They look good in their organization for having hired such an excellent speaker.

- They want others in their company to BENEFIT from your program just as their division did.

Do not miss this opportunity to get REFERRALS.

Using Sponsors

A sponsor is an organization which offers your presentation under their auspices. They take all the risks i.e. promoting, advertising, design, printing of brochure etc. Great way for you to establish credibility.

NOTES

NOTES

KNOW YOUR AUDIENCE

Ask yourself... '*What do they expect to get out of my program or speech?*" and "*what is their motivation for attending this program?*"

What is the purpose of the convention? They might say that it is to motivate their people to sell TWICE as much as they did last year. Remember this: whatever they want, that's YOUR specialty! You can usually adjust your presentation to fit the needs of the clients.

The participant's reasons for attending your program can be broken down into several factors that encompass these two basic needs:

- A desire to learn more about the subject matter.

- A desire to earn more money.

- A desire to change an unwanted behaviour pattern

- Career change.

- Individual or group management.
- Individual is required to take your program

Preparing Your Introduction And Closing

Whenever you speak you should have someone introduce you and close with a brief message.

Your conclusion should be powerful. This could be a story of a personal experience that creates a highly emotionally charged feeling in your audience. You want them to remember you and you want to create good feelings. You want them to invest in your products which are offered for sale in the back of the room after your presentation.

Answering Questions

It is important to keep a balance between participation and control. You want them to participate but you don't want them to control the program. From time to time you will find such a person. If that is the case, tell that individual that you would be happy to spend time with them later in order to answer all their questions. Remember, try and get others to become involved.

NOTES

Awarding Certificates

It's good public relations because participants usually frame them and hang them on the wall.

How to Handle a Dissatisfied Participant

Have a standard money back guarantee. However, have your 'dissatisfied participant' stay for the ENTIRE program, this eliminates making judgements about the program before they have heard the entire presentation.

TAPE RECORDING YOUR PRESENTATION

This is a personal preference. However, you may want to sell your OWN RECORDINGS of your live presentations as another means of generating income.

Some speakers do not allow participants recording any or all of

NOTES

their presentation. If this is your preference, make sure you advise your audience as well as the booking agent / speaker's bureau that you are booking through.

THE VENUE

Selecting And Renting Meeting Rooms

- Location is the number one priority.

- Ample parking.

- Quality vs. price (go first class if you can afford it).

    Some suggestions:

    ▸ Deal directly with the hotel yourself.

    ▸ Contact the sales or catering office when you make your meeting room reservation.

    ▸ Request less space than you need. If you get more people they can usually put you in a larger room.

    ▸ Check arrangements when you arrive.

NOTES

Seating Arrangements

- Theatre style.

- School room style (will hold about half the people than theatre style. For more suggestions on seating styles, see page 94).

- Chairs - are they comfortable?

- Will they need to take notes?

Audio Visual

Audio-visual equipment, i.e. over-head projectors (OHP), computer projection, TV & VCR/DVD, audio equipment, may come as an extra charge in most hotel. In most cases flip charts and chalk boards are included in your rental cost of the room.

Serving Coffee

Coffee is a pain in the a**! It's expensive but people expect it.

In-house Meals

Depending upon the location you may wish to include meals. Remember to bill this into your tuition fee. Another thing to worry about: people on special diets. However, it gives people an opportunity to mix, exchange and share.

NOTES

NOTES

PAYING YOUR BILL

Always check it – pay for only what you requested. And pay on time: avoid all interests charges and bad credit ratings. Keep all receipts: they may be tax-deductable.

PUBLISHING AND MARKETING YOUR OWN PRODUCTS

To be financially successful in the speaking and seminar business, you must have "PRODUCTS".

If you do not have "products" to sell you will miss out on a substantial portion of your potential income.

The Monograph

A monograph is 10 to 20 double spaced typed pages bound in an attractive cover. The printing cost is very inexpensive, the title should correspond with the subject matter of your speech or seminar. Your cost, less than $1.00 per piece, you sell $2 to

$10 each (UK less than 50 pence per piece, you sell £1 to £5 each).

Your First Book

The next step is to write a book that is related to your subject matter. Your book will not only make money for you but it will add to your credibility, image and prestige. The best way to write a book is to write two or three pages a day, no more, no less.

Once written, find a professional to "look and read it over".

The next step is to have your book published (or publish it yourself).

Tape Cassettes or CD's

Tape cassettes and specially CD's have the HIGHEST profit margin of any product you can sell as a speaker. A general rule of thumb is that each cassette or CD should be priced for no less than $10 each (£5.00 UK).

How do you go about putting together your cassettes or CD's?

First, you must write a script. Find a reliable studio for recording. They charge by the hour. In addition, find out if there are "editing charges", will

NOTES

they "package" it for you, do they have the expertise?

More questions to consider:

- How fast can you produce my tapes?

- How many cassettes do I have to buy at a time?

- Will you ship them?

- What kind of packaging do you offer?

- What is your charge per tape, per album, etc.

Selling Your Products

Ok, you know have your own products ready for sale. Whatever you sell, make sure it is packaged attractively.

Now, concentrate on the quality of your presentation and use a SOFT SELL for your products, you will have much better results. Don't forget to use Master Card and Visa to increase your product sales. Charge cards will add 20% to 30% increase in sales.

NOTES

NOTES

It helps to offer a FREE gift that will be given away at your book table. One printed sheet with some helpful hints, a poem, etc.

You can increase your sales by offering books by other authors on the same or related subjects. Remember to inclose an order forms of all your products and services.

Always distribute an order form to your participants after the project is over.
Or mail them one at a later date.
Keep your name, service and products "alive".

"HOW TO GET IN MAIL ORDER" by Melvin Power is an excellent read for those wishing to get their feet wet.

In every city there are dozens of DIRECT SALES ORGANIZATIONS such as Shaklee, Amway, Nulife, Tupperware, Mary Kay Cosmetics etc. <u>Those groups of people found in EVERY city can be a tremendous source of income.</u>

If marketed properly, they can be a tremendous source of income to the PROFESSIONAL SPEAKER. The advantage of working with these organizations is that they are located in virtually every city. You can do back-to-back speaking engagements, and hopefully, travel the complete circuit. If they like your program and they like YOU as a person, they will promote you to others within their organization on a nationwide basis.

Your success in working with these organizations will be in the direct proportion to the trust level you have built with them.

NOTES

THE FIRST YEAR AS A PROFESSIONAL SPEAKER

Most organizations are reluctant to hire speakers who have little experience. But how are you going to have speaking experience if no one will allow you speak? The answer is to SPEAK FOR FREE!

This is your on the job training (so to speak!?!)

First, contact as many organizations as possible (using the procedures outlined in this book). Offer a mini or a one hour seminar. In your proposal letter mention that you are so confident they will be satisfied with your presentation that they will want to book you at a future date for your regular seminar.

Be sure to sell the BENEFITS of your free mini-seminar.

Your brochure or flyer should state what BENEFITS the participants will gain from attending your presentation. In return for all this you are asking that they promote your min-seminar and turn out an audience of 100 or more people.

You may be wondering, "How can I make money speaking for free?" Simple, if you haven't figured it out already, your income will be derived from the sale of your books and tapes. To turn your mini-seminar into DOLLARS you will have to effectively market your tapes and books.

Have special seminar packages for mini-seminars, i.e. one tape, say $10.00 and one book say $7.95 - offer this as a "Special" for $16.00 - this will give your participants incentive to purchase BOTH items rather than having them as two separate ones.

Your mini-seminar must be highly MOTIVATIONAL. Your subject matter must be presented in such a way that the audience will WANT MORE THAN JUST A MINI-SEMINAR.

Have three or four speeches you know well and that have been polished and perfected. Tailor it to the needs of your participants.

Russell Conwell gave his speech "Acres of Diamonds" over 50,000 times! Many speakers have the same speech, the only change is the title.

Your intention should not be to sell them on the program but to sell YOU. It's YOU they really want.

NOTES

Explain that your seminar package will help them to accomplish certain specifics covered in your presentation. Give a few examples of what information is on the tape.

Plan on giving at LEAST TWO seminars a week - keep your name alive and VISIBLE. Have enough confidence in yourself to accept that you can do it. Don't settle for less. Remember, TWO SPEECHES A WEEK. Make it your number one goal.

Do this for one year and you'll be on the road to fame and fortune in the speaking and seminar business. Believe in YOURSELF and others will believe in you. Soon, people will be asking YOU to speak because you will be well known in the speaking profession.

Remember, the only obstacle is procrastination, and you can eliminate that by STARTING NOW.

NOTES

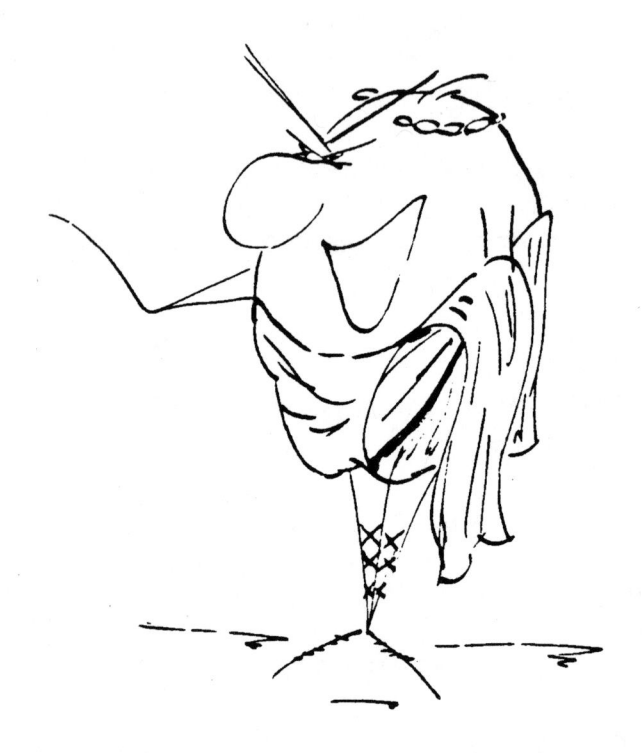

Super, super success and sincere best wishes.

Paul P. Talbot

International Speaker

www.dialaspeaker.com

SAMPLE SPEAKING AGREEMENT

Name of Organization: ....

Name of Person to Contact: ....

Title: ....

Address: ....

Business Phone #: ....

Other Phone #: ....

Program will be held at (address): ....

Name of Nearest Major Airport: ....

Title of Seminar or Speech: ....

Presentation date(s): .... Time(s) .....

Length of Speech/Seminar: ....

Estimated Attendance: ....

Terms of Agreement: .... Fee: .....

Expenses: ....

Tape/Book Sales:

I will make my tapes and books available to the program participants. For advance shipment of these materials, the person who will be responsible for receiving them is:

Name: .... Address: ....

City: .... Province: ....

Postal Code: ....

Telephone: Business: .... Home: ....

There will be NO tape recording or filming of the presentation without prior written consent.

Minimum period for CANCELLATION of this agreement is .... days prior to the program date. Failure to cancel within this period will impose a cancellation fee of $ .... unless the speaker is able to re-book the above date(s).

So that your dates may be GUARANTEED, a signed copy of this agreement must be returned to this office within 10 days.

Authorized Signature (Organization) ....

Date: ....

Speaker / Organization: ....

Date: ....

Just a Few Questions

... ABOUT THE PRINCIPAL CONTACT:

Name: .... Title: ....

Company Name: ....

Address: ....

City: .... Postal Code: ....

Business Telephone: .... Other: ....

....

... ABOUT THE GROUP:

Name of Group: ....

Number of People: ....

Brief Description of Group: ....

Audience Description (job, concerns, experience, etc.) ....

....

... ABOUT THE PROGRAM:

Date: .... Time: ....

Address/Building: ....

Directions to get there: ....

....

Objectives for My Presentation should be: . . . .

. . . .

. . . .

... ABOUT MY PREPARATION:

Could you send me a Group Brochure,
Newsletter, Program Announcement, etc.?

How did you hear about me? . . . .

. . . .

Suggestions / Requests / Questions? . . . .

. . . .

. . . .

. . . .

Stay Enthusiastic, Paul P. Talbot

HOW TO FACILITATE WITH FACTS, FEELINGS AND FUN©

A practical how-to book on facilitating your own workshop or seminar

NOTES

SIX WAYS TO MAKE THIS COURSE MORE VALUABLE

- **Participate** to engage your learning
- **Question** to enhance your learning
- **Read** to expand your learning
- **Reflect** to measure your learning
- **Apply** to transfer your learning
- **Innovate** to adapt your learning

Tell me - I forget
Show me - I remember
Involve me - I understand

... Chinese Proverb

First remember you are the EXPERT in your given subject or topic. You MUST believe in you FIRST, otherwise you will project this to your participants. Once you have made the decision that you are the expert, your confidence level will increase and you will begin to feel more in control.

Presenting any workshop or seminar can be very nerve racking, but, at the same time, it can be so invigorating and you feel on a real 'high' knowing that you have something worthwhile to share.

Once you have perfected your topic, there are many areas where you can start to generate an income (see "Sources of Speaker Income" on the next page). However, remember that each and every one of us started small, usually by doing it for FREE until we established a name for ourselves or until someone offered to PAY US. This manual is to support and encourage you.

Good luck!

Paul Talbot

NOTES

SOURCES OF SPEAKER INCOME

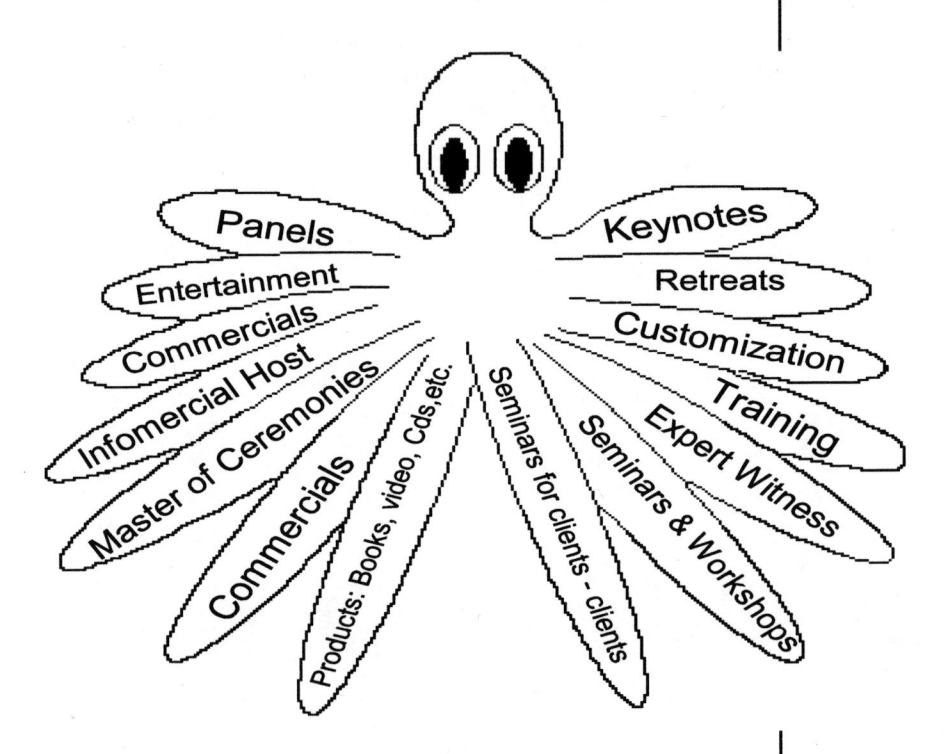

- Panels
- Entertainment
- Commercials
- Infomercial Host
- Master of Ceremonies
- Commercials
- Products: Books, video, Cds, etc.
- Seminars for clients - clients
- Keynotes
- Retreats
- Customization
- Training
- Expert Witness
- Seminars & Workshops

If you are running your own public workshops you would have mailed out your own brochure, posters and news releases. Hopefully you have included mailing out to newspapers, TV and radio stations - many offer "Community Announcements": you should create yourself a mailing list and send out info on a regular basis. If possible, get in depth interviews, either on radio or TV stations or with a local newspaper reporter - any coverage is better than none.

You have selected the venue (make sure that it is appealing and is the right atmosphere for your workshop / seminar).

Now that you have received the registration forms as well as the appropriate workshop/seminar fee (in some cases you may wish to consider a siding scale) it is now the actual presentation day.

Get there early. Cheek room layout, if necessary change it to suit the needs of the participants.

PREPARATION SAVES THE DAY

On a black board, white board or flip chart, write...

- the name of topic / subject

- your name and phone number

- the class times if this is on-going

- the objectives of the course / topic

- an agenda, if need be

Preparation Checklist

✓ Set up registration table, have registration list.

✓ If possible, have someone else do cheek-in and registration of participants.

✓ Provide name tags.

✓ Have tables set-up with water jugs and glasses available as well as coffee / tea if you are supplying same.

✓ If no lunch or meals provided in the course fee, ensure that eating establishments are close by.

✓ Parking - does the hotel supply it and at what cost?

✓ Handouts - make sure that you have enough copies for everyone including any late comers that might arrive (searching for a photocopier is not very professional, anticipate the unexpected).

✓ Coat racks if needed.

Equipment

Depending upon the size of the group and the topic, some facilitators may

NOTES

choose to have some equipment to assist them.

Whatever you are going to use make sure that you have checked it out and you know how it works.

Let's start with the basics:

- ✓ pens and pencils

- ✓ loose leaf paper

- ✓ card stock (if required)

- ✓ 3-ring binders (some facilitators supply same)

- ✓ high lighters and/or markers

Other

- ✓ computer screen projector, VCR, video camera, TV, blank tapes – perhaps have someone else to handle this

- ✓ chalks and black boards or dry-erase markers and white boards (make sure you have the dry-erase type for the white board! The permanent is for flip charts **ONLY!**)

- ✓ flip chart paper and stand

- ✓ access to copier, if necessary

- ✓ OHP – overhead projector

NOTES

NOTES

If you are using overhead transparencies, please make sure that your wording is large enough for people to see and read at the back of the room (I once worked with someone that used a regular typewriter to type their information, with 200 plus people in the room, beyond row four the words were just a blur). <u>Always check it out</u>! Put yourself in the other person's seat.

LET THE SHOW BEGIN

Welcome

As the facilitator it is your role to welcome everyone. Give them an overview of the workshop: refer to the topics on the board. This let them know what will be covered each week.

If this is a one day workshop, some form of Agenda should be written on the board, giving people an idea of what will be covered.

Background of The Facilitator

You may have a handout for this which gives details in depth, but I feel it is necessary for you, or someone else, to give a short bio on who you are, what you have done and why you are qualified to speak today.

If you were introduced by someone else, you may now wish to add something else: this helps break down fears and warm up the room.

House Keeping Information

Give details on the washrooms nearest you, fire exits as well as fire drill procedures.

Recording equipment – do you allow them to be used by participants?

Ground Rules

If your group is relatively small, you may ask the participants to self introduce, i.e. their name, what they hope to get out of the presentation or why they are there – modify it to suit the needs of those attending.

If it is too large a group for that, then when they are seated at tables, ask them to make a name plate. This makes it much easier and more personal for the facilitator and all participants.

Again depending upon the type of program you are conducting this may or may not apply.

NOTES

Here are some examples of Ground Rules:

- Confidentiality
- Trust
- Openness
- One person to speak at a time
- Challenge the facilitator, if need be
- No bad language
- Do not judge others
- Respect
- Have fun

Have the group add their own. Make a copy of the Ground Rules and give to each person, this way you can refer to them on an on-going basis.

Coffee and Lunch breaks - agree as a team, if possible.

Tailoring Your Agenda

As you have already given them the Agenda or Objectives of the course you might, if you so wish, ask them what they would like you to cover. This can be done after a break or after you have covered a certain area or topic.

NOTES

Often, it gives the participants an opportunity to expand the area with questions that relate to their own particular concerns. Always keep the communication flowing two ways, from them to you and visa versa.

MONITOR YOURSELF

Remember, even though you know your subject matter, it maybe your PERSONALITY that carries the course / workshop.

Ask yourself the following questions:

- Are you friendly?
- Are you informative?
- Do you listen to others?
- Do you give constructive feedback?
- Do you know how to reflect and paraphrase?

When you are trying very hard to keep everyone interested, alert and hopefully, awake, it is necessary that you know how to pace yourself and to speak at different levels and speed in

NOTES

order that you do not come across boring or monotonous.

If you have NEVER taken any speaking courses I would suggest that you tape yourself, playback and listen, then ask the question: *"would you pay to listen to you?"*

Remember, practice does make perfect but you don't want to come across too rehearsed: You want to come across natural. Allow for flexibility: you never know what kind of question you will be asked. Be spontaneous for this will "just happen". And always speak from the heart.

Watch the Participants

As you look around the room, ask yourself...

- Are they interested?

- Do they look bored?

- Do they look half asleep?

- Are they looking around the room and not at you?

- Are they doodling on paper?

If any of the above are happening, they are "tuning" you out and you need to bring them back into the group. Ask

NOTES

a question and direct it to that person, or, ask for an opinion or suggestion, again, direct it to that person.

If you have given them handouts earlier in the course, you will often find that people will just start reading. Tell the group that you have handouts for this section and that they need not take notes but handouts will be given out later on in the course, or at the end of the session.

Remember, you will have "talkers" and others that will sit back and not participate or contribute in anyway.

- Are they talking to someone else?

- Are they staring into space?

You do not want to embarrass them but you do want to bring them back into the group. You can ask them a simple question or give a response yourself to a situation and then ask someone in the group for their contribution. Using myself as an example takes the pressure off of the more quiet people in the group.

Also, make sure that you ask more than ONE person (other than the person that appears to be disinterested). This way it does not seem that you are "picking" on just that person.

NOTES

As the facilitator, it is up to you to set the tone and try to achieve participation from everyone.

Feedback

You need to confirm on an on-going basis that the participants understand what you are saying and that their needs are being met. Give an example, like: *"I started clearing my clutter by..."*

Next, go around the room (again, depending upon the size of the group) and ask each person for their ideas, suggestions, examples etc. If someone "cannot think" at this time, say you will come back to them later on, do not pressure them, but feedback for the facilitator is vital, you need to know that you are reaching your participants and that what you are saying has value and purpose.

Pace Yourself

You need to balance the amount of time that you have been allocated for this workshop, taking into account coffee and lunch breaks. Pacing yourself is vital as you want to allow enough time to cover all of the material without feeling "rushed".

NOTES

If you are conducting an evening or half day workshop you may choose only two topics, this can be done by the participants. Get each person to write out the topic of their choice, place them all in a box and get them to take out only two, next session repeat the process.

Keeping Them Interested

This can be an on-going challenge but it is important that you try and maintain the interest of the group. As we said earlier, asking for feedback or enrolling the participation of a volunteer in the group is one way. You may also wish to break the large group down into smaller ones, let them elect a spokesperson or recorder (secretary). Give each group a question or situation (it may be the same for all of them or something different for each group), give them sufficient time to come up with their suggestions and then re-group as one. The representative will then present the findings of the group. Ask the group as a whole for any further feedback and then ask the remaining groups for their comments (this is, if the other groups have the same question / topic) if not, get the next group to present their question / topic.

NOTES

This enables the participants to get to know each other (in smaller group size). Remember to PRAISE each group for their contribution.

Conducting a One Day Workshop

Prior to the breaks, ask for feedback or give them something to think about during the break. You need to keep the group interested and, at the same time, on track.

Conducting On-going Evening Sessions

At the start of the evening, you may wish to give a short overview of the previous week and ask for any feedback, or go around the room (if you have a manageable size group) and ask for progress on "clearing their clutter" in the last week, or a question applicable to the topic. Again, this will be governed by the topic, type and length of the workshop or course that you are giving.

After the break, before you progress, you may ask them something like, *"What useful ideas and suggestions have you been able to put into practice so far?"*.

NOTES

Again, you may wish to share your own "clutter" solution, or ask someone in the group to expand on their previous suggestions / ideas: i.e. *"Mary, last week you shared with the group how you started clearing out your bedroom closet, have you made any progress and what other changes, if any, have you made?"*

Educate, Inform and Entertain

Your participants want to leave with something, that can be:

- useful information (you asked them the question)

- handouts that have purpose and value

- need to be motivated, so they come back

- briefly outline what you will cover next week (if this is an on-going course)

- perhaps get them to think about a project they can work on

- get them to write up their own Action Plan

NOTES

NOTES

- get them to commit to paper their goals as it relates to this course

- each week get them to give feedback on the status of their project (i.e. clearing the clutter) this is NOT a contest, do not make them feel guilty if they do NOTHING

- have fun

It is important to remember the course content must be *INTERESTING, EDUCATIONAL and ENTERTAINING.* People want to be inspired, they want to learn, and it is your job to motivate them.

Closing

Allow enough time for you to answer any questions or concerns that your participants may have. Also, at the end of all courses, you should have each participant complete an EVALUATION FORM (see enclosed sample on page 107).

You may wish to close the day by going around the room to each person and ask what one thing they found particularly useful. Depending upon the mood of the group, you may even suggest to have a Hug Circle.

This is also an opportunity for you to talk about any new workshops that you have coming up, you may wish to bring your own brochure and leave for each person to pick up, if they so wish.

Finally, as the facilitator, you want to THANK THEM for their being there and for their contribution throughout the day. You may suggest that they can phone you should any questions come up later.

Evaluation Forms

The Evaluations will vary from person to person, read them (if that is allowed) or ask for them at a later date. Be constructive and do not take the information personally. Some people will want more handouts, breaks etc. but you are one person and can only do your very best. Learn from them, make changes, if necessary and above all, have fun yourself.

NOTES

EXCEPTIONS

NOTES

Hopefully all will go smoothly. But, some glitches might occur. Try and be prepared. How will you handle the following:

Lateness and Absenteeism

Will you let people stream in when ever they are ready, will you wait a maximum of 15 minutes, will you start on time, no matter what?

If your course is on-going you may wish to establish a procedure for those persons that are away. They may call you and advise you that they will be unable to attend on _____ due to _____ . Common courtesy and respect for EACH OTHER is important.

Disruptions

Often you will get "talkers" in the group that will try and disrupt the group, you need to watch them and perhaps during the break, bring this to their attention. Do not try to show them up, perhaps use humour and at the same time, get your point across.

If this is an on-going course you can always telephone them at home and discuss the situation. It is important that you let them know that you value their contribution but as a facilitator you have a responsibility to the whole group.

NOTES

THE HANDBOOK©

NOTES

Before we get started let me ask you a question;

"Do you feel <u>passionate</u> and <u>confident</u> about your subject matter?"

If the answer is "yes" then let's move ahead. If you are unsure, then you need to spend more time practising and fine tuning your craft.

As a speaker, we have all given FREE presentations, but there comes a time when we must move ahead and start charging for our knowledge, skills and experience.

First, are you going to offer a SEMINAR or a WORKSHOP? Do you know the difference? Will your presentation be all "chalk and talk" or will it be "interactive"

If you are still at the stage where you are giving FREE presentations then take the time, effort and energy to use them wisely.

First, have a friend RECORD all of your presentations. This will then give you an opportunity to review them, make changes, perhaps add humour (if needed) and to become more confident with your presentations.

Here are eleven LIFE LESSONS taken from page 27 of PROFIT, APRIL 2000 issue.

Success Secrets from Canada's Entrepreneurial Pathfinders.

- Be passionate about what you choose to do.

- Define you niche and develop specialized products that add value.

- Enter a growing market. That growth could finance your mistakes.

- Choose your partners wisely. Make sure they supply skills that you don't have.

- Start small and grow carefully.

- Stick to the basics; understand your clients' needs and satisfy them.

- Hire the best employees.

- Exceed your clients' expectations.

- Develop strategic partnerships.

- Remember, everything takes longer and costs more than you estimated.

NOTES

GO FOR IT!   NOTES

As the expert in your given field, let's now take a look at planning the Workshop/Seminar.

Who would the topic appeal to?

When would you offer the event?:

- ❏ If during the day, is it the kind of subject matter that people would take the day off?

- ❏ Evenings – this is great but consider the fact that many people have already put in a full day so is 7 p.m. to 10 p.m. too long?

- ❏ Weekends – which day would be the best and would one evening and one full day on the weekend be ideal?

The questions you need to ask yourself are: *"Who would attend my workshop, how can I reach them"* and *"would they pay?"*

You may choose to offer your workshop/seminar through an organization or professional association (refer to the Yellow Pages and match your subject matter with like-minded associations that need you).

The association or professional group may be responsible for the brochure, venue and registration.

As the presenter, you may either receive a flat fee, or a fee plus percentage for number of attendees.

By allowing someone else to handle the event it takes the full risk from you, but the profit to you may not be as much. Again, the decision is yours.

While conducting your workshops, make sure to:

- Have all events <u>recorded</u>. You can review your presentation skills and you can use the tape as a promotional vehicle for others wishing to use your services.

- Have a friend take "live" photographs of you in action – you may choose to use them in your own brochure and promotional materials (Ask the participants who may appear on the photos for their permission).

Let's Get Started!

You have decided upon the day and date. You have already received packages of information from several hotels. These packages include details

NOTES

of all rooms, sizes, layouts as well as full details on meals.

Depending on the number of people attending your workshop/seminar, you need to think about the layout.

Will it be:

- ❏ Classroom Style
- ❏ Theatre Style
- ❏ Boardroom Style
- ❏ Banquet Style
- ❏ Hollow Square
- ❏ U-Shape
- ❏ T-Shape

Remember that when people have a "day out", they like to be treated, I think, in a special way. Therefore the venue must reflect this. Have a WELCOME table and name tags for each person, a coat rack close by, and make sure the washrooms are well marked and easily accessible. If you are using tables, please make sure that water jugs and glasses are placed so that people can get to them easily.

Refer to page 77 of "*How to Facilitate with Facts, Feelings and Fun*©" regarding introduction of the speaker and general housekeeping rules.

Setting up the room is very important and necessary to have all items available to the participants. Please see page 74 For complete details, in the section entitled: "Equipment".

NOTES

As you progress obtaining more speaking engagements, see page 72 on Sources of Speaker Income in the workbook "*How to Facilitate with Facts, Feelings and Fun*©". As you give more speeches or workshops, you will find that your name will grow and new and exciting doors will open for you.

I want to take some time to talk about "<u>IMAGE</u>". I have made the mistake of putting together brochures and other documentation that looked somewhat unprofessional, at the time thinking I was saving money. I now know from experience that you only get ONE chance to make a good impression so make sure that it is a PROFESSIONAL one. Have your photograph or logo on ALL your materials and make them look nice. Please, tie this in with your letterhead and business cards.

Most speakers work from their home so consider the following:

- Fax – a dedicated line.

- Computer and printer.

- Copy machine (or access to one)

- Printing Supplies

- Answering Machine or Voicemail

- Email

NOTES

Remember to tie in your logo / photograph as well as colour of stationary, business cards, presentation folders, thank-you cards, etc.

Before you come up with an amount to charge your participants, please think about the following costs:

- Room rental for the day

- Buffet lunch or?

- Coffee / tea – usually extra, per cup

- Service charges

- Goods & Services Tax (check the local taxation laws)

Take into account the cost of design and printing of your brochure and handout materials for the day, as well as postage and any advertising you may do.

You may wish to see what your competition is charging or what the market will bear.

Once you have decided upon all these factors then you will need to mail out your brochures. Allow a 4-6 week lead time prior to the actual date. In the meantime, prepare news releases and try to obtain coverage on radio and TV. Many newspapers have a section on Community Events or their

NOTES

own Business Calendar, try and get the information included but again, there is no guarantee.

Look very closely at your local newspapers, select the section whereby you feel your topic would fit in, call the reporter and see about getting a personal interview. Free publicity, especially if you are able to get your photograph included and details of your upcoming workshop is worth a great deal of money and, you can reproduce the article and mail it to all future enquiries or give to participants of your workshops.

FREE GIVE-AWAY(S)

As my main topic is "Clutter" I wrote a poem which has been reproduced on card stock and ready for framing or photocopying to give to others. This poem I send out and give away with all my communications. Why? It is a constant reminder of what I do and offer, interestingly, people like it and ask for it.

The poem is also sent out with our news release (see sample news release on page 102), in "*How to Facilitate with Facts, Feelings and Fun*©"

NOTES

NOTES

Wether you are booking yourself or using the services of a Speakers Bureau, you will need either a Contract or a Letter of Agreement (Samples are available: See page 65). Remember, a Speakers Bureau will receive a commission to be paid from your standard fee (this is usually 25%).

Most speakers usually ask for 50% of the fee prior to the engagement, this will depend on how well you know your client.

Prior to your booking you may wish to carry out a preprogram questionnaire. This will give you an idea of who would be attending, spouses invited, age range (if necessary), names, job titles, expectations of the clients, challenges faced by the people attending, follow-up.

SPEAKER PRODUCTS

As time progresses you may wish to consider your own products, this could range from workbooks, books, tapes, tote bags, key rings, just to name a few. People like to take things with them and it gives them the opportunity to review the topic in their own home or office.

Back of Room Sales can be VERY lucrative. Have a friend "working" for you, be there to sign or personalize the materials.

By self publishing your own materials (waiting for a publisher to go with your book / materials may take some time) you may have a bigger investment but a higher rate of profit.

Arrange to take credit cards. Become a merchant. You will double your sales. One speaker told me about 90% of all sales are on credit cards.

Offer a percentage of your sales to the group so that all may benefit. Consider offering a flat fee per person, include the workbook (obtain a low rate from the printer for volume) and the "X" amount, per person, back to the organization (if it is a non-profit, charitable designation).

Consider an organization that has a membership of 2,000 persons – how do you reach them, do you have something to offer that they could use? Think about it, be creative.

Give awards or consider an Annual Reunion. Each year we hold our Reunion for Clutterers and participants of our Voluntary Simplicity workshops with guest speakers, updates, new products and our own Newsletter.

NOTES

Team up with others, with topics that compliment each other. Start your own newsletter, publish upcoming events, trade with other like-minded people.

Monthly Support Groups: As part of our service we offer a monthly support group, this is led by dedicated people, with a local contact number.

Study each piece of mail, newspapers, magazines, etc. This is one way of building up your mailing lists. Ask yourself "*How can I help this company, or refer to this company?* "

Collect brochures of all your competition, study their format, style, layout, design, cost of the workshop (what does it include?) and where are they conducting the workshop. Do they project a professional image or does it look second class? Would you pay for this workshop? Ask yourself "*What are the benefits I would receive by attending this workshop?*"

By becoming the "**expert**" in your given field you could then consider offering consulting services.

NOTES

Handouts

NOTES

- Example of News Release/Press Release (page 102)

- Suggested Bio – example: "About the Author" (page 103)

- Facilitator's record of participants personal information and progress (have participants complete the TOP part only, page 106)

- Feedback Form (page 107)

- Comments from Participants (page 109)

- Sample of Workshop Poster and Flyer (pages 112 and 113)

From Paul Talbot

News Release

FOR IMMEDIATE RELEASE
Contact: Paul Talbot (604) 684-5059

Taken the "Clutter" course but now lack the drive motivation and energy to get back on track? Help is at hand. You need to attend the <u>SECOND ANNUAL REUNION</u>, a "must" for all clutterers that are **STUCK**; Paul Talbot, creator and founder of <u>"Clear the Clutter and Simplify Your Life©"</u> speaks on ...

"Don't give up, today could be the day!"
He will share with you time-tested ways of overcoming the clutter and chaos in your life and, how to maintain it. This one day exciting workshop will be held on:

Saturday March 25, 2000 from 10 a.m. to 3:30 p.m., Fraser Room, Best Western Hotel, 1755 Davie Street, Vancouver, BC (parking available)

... and will include:

- Introduction of new facilitators
- Details on our new Website
- Monthly Support Groups
- Workbooks now available

- Meet our Executive Organizer
- Networking "Clutter" table
- Launch of our own association
- Door prizes

If you are interested in clearing the clutter from your life or just wanting to bring about Voluntary Simplicity, then this Reunion will give you direction and clarity. For complete details call: Paul Talbot (604) 684-5059

-30-

note: -30- stands for "the end" or "end of story"

About the Author

More than an author, he is a trainer, simplicity coach, clutter therapist and certified Job Club Facilitator. His enthusiasm, laughter and passion for life are the keys to his personality. Since his personal experience with cancer in November 1998, he has again re-evaluated and simplified his life further.

Background / Experience:

Senior Lecturer/Programme Director at Central University, Birmingham, England; Instructor at Vancouver Community College; Instructor for Continuing Education for the Vancouver and New Westminster School Boards, Langara College and the West End Community Centre. He also worked as a Private Secretary / Personal Assistant in London, England and Tripoli, Libya.

Paul owned and operated his own Personnel / Employment Agency for nine years in Vancouver, BC, and has worked for many non-profit agencies including: The Vancouver Friends for Life Society (he was Program Director / Facilitator / Counsellor) and was co-founder of the HIV First Step Support Group / Program.

As a certified Job Club Facilitator helping unemployed adults, Paul was facilitator / co-ordinator at Gordon Neighbourhood House and facilitator at the Immigrant Services Society and at the YMCA.

Paul completes his HIV/AIDS Training at Aidsline, Birmingham, England and has volunteered in this area for many years offering support, counselling and facilitation of groups.

Accomplishments:

He has written and published several books, newsletters and articles worldwide. He is co-author of the North American book "TEELINE Shorthand", and included in "Positive Power People" published by Royal Publishing, California, USA. He is creator / founder of the CLUTTER series which includes: "Clear the Clutter and Simplify Your Life©", "Clear the Clutter for Seniors©", "Simple and Forgotten Things – Voluntary Simplicity©", and "Be a Winner, Steps to Success©". Paul has other books he is working on as well as audio presentation.

Paul has appeared on the CBCTV, Studio 4 and Plugged In for SHAW TV, BCTV, City Pulse TV as well as CBC Radio, Early Edition and CKNW with Rafe Mair. He has been featured in the Vancouver Sun, Vancouver Courier, Georgia Straight, Shared Vision, Burnaby Newsleader, Family Circle, and the Globe & Mail.

He has been a keynote speaker for many conferences and in-company presentations, and continues to share his skills, knowledge and life-long experiences with others.

His unique style reflects his sense of humour, his caring and his support of others as well as his "gifted" way of communicating.

He lives and loves life to the fullest and his passion is helping others reach and fulfil their dreams.

Mission Statement:

To help individuals and organizations release their full potential by providing the means for training and developing opportunities.

Vision:

A healthy world of well-balanced people who function by inspiring one another daily to greater heights and depths of love, joy, harmony and co-creativity.

Commitment:

To offer an atmosphere of freedom and inspiration to support you sharing the gift of who you really are.

| Facilitator's record of participants personal information and progress. |

Name: _____   Today's Date: _____

Address: _____   Receipt #: _____

Phone#: _____

Facilitators Comments

Dates Attending: _____

Name: _____   Today's Date: _____

Address: _____   Receipt #: _____

Phone#: _____

Facilitators Comments

Dates Attending: _____

Course Evaluation

In order to provide you with the best program possible, we would appreciate your answers to the following questions. A staff member will collect this sheet or you can return it to the facilitator. Thank you.

Course Name: **Date:**

	Yes	Partially	No
1. Is the content of the course what you expected based on the course description in the brochure?	___	___	___
2. Is the course topic being covered to your satisfaction?	___	___	___
3. Would you recommend this course to a friend?	___	___	___

	Excellent	Good	Fair	Poor
4. Please rate the quality of instruction.	___	___	___	___
5. The facilities are ...	___	___	___	___
6. I would rate the service, courtesy and friendliness of the staff as...	___	___	___	___

What did you like best about the course?

_____

_____

What suggestions do you have for improving the course?

_____

_____

Other comments:

_____

_____

_____

May we use your comments in our brochure or other publicity about our program? | Yes | | No |

If yes, please sign   _____
                       (Signature)

COMMENTS FROM PARTICIPANTS OF PAUL TALBOT'S "CLEAR THE CLUTTER AND SIMPLICITY WORKSHOPS"

"A lively, humorous presentation that motivates."

– Tony Sainsbury

"Thank you for your warmth and support to us and your useful suggestions." – Sue M.

"Excellent speaker; lots of good ideas."

"Everything was clear and understandable."

"The content was just what I wanted."

"Paul Talbot was excellent, clear and to the point with lots of humour and ideas. A very enjoyable day."

"Subject covered thoroughly and clearly."

"Very good course."

"Good pace, opportunities given for questions. Paul's extremely personable, humourous. Thank you."

"Wonderful suggestions to get us started."

"Paul Talbot is an excellent speaker, very humourous."

"Down to earth, realistic, fun, a good start for me."

"Motivating."

"It was very focussed, reinforced things I already knew and some new ideas to put into practice."

"Paul Talbot's delivery and style made the course more interesting and human."

"Paul has a wonderfully pleasing demeanor, great sense of humour. He has a great voice and knows how to use it. Very easy to listen to."

"I really wasn't looking forward to spending Saturday in class, but I found it very interesting and valuable."

"Fun, thoughtful, informative and entertaining."

To find out more about Paul's services, log on to www.dialaspeaker.com

VANCOUVER COMMUNITY COLLEGE

July 9, 2004

Mr. Paul Talbot
P.O. Box 404, 1195 Davie Street
Vancouver, B.C. V6E 1N2

To Whom It May Concern:

Mr. Paul Talbot, whom your organization may be considering to present a workshop, asked me if I would be interested and willing to write a letter of recommendation.

As Human Resources Coordinator, Employee Development at Vancouver Community College, I am pleased to share my personal and professional views. I contacted Mr. Talbot to learn more about his background, knowledge and experience with a topic that he is well known to offer "De-cluttering – whether it is for your personal or professional life".

I found Mr. Talbot was more than accommodating when making arrangements to present two different workshops for our employees. He came to the workshops well prepared and eager to share his knowledge and expertise on the subject matter. He has the gift of making all the participants feel welcome and comfortable in the way he sets the environment for his presentation.

It was clearly evident the passion Mr. Talbot has for the subject matter. Not only did he share his knowledge but he did so in a very confident, engaging and humorous manner. Mr. Talbot draws on his personal experiences or shares pertinent stories to get his point across. The workshops were very interactive and participants were welcome and encouraged to participate either by sharing their viewpoints or asking questions specific to their needs.

I look forward to inviting Mr. Talbot to return to Vancouver Community College to offer additional workshops throughout the year. A number of our employees have requested support in this area and based on evaluation feedback from both workshops, I feel confident that Mr. Talbot is the ideal person to continue to meet the needs of our employees.

I believe your employees will benefit from having the opportunity of attending one or more of Mr. Talbot's presentations.

Yours truly,

Carol Sicoli

Carol Sicoli
HR Coordinator, Employee Development

○ City Centre Campus: 250 W. Pender Street, Vancouver, B.C. V6B 1S9 Tel:(604) 443-8300 Fax:(604) 443-8588
○ King Edward Campus: 1155 E. Broadway, Box 24620, Stn. F, Vancouver, B.C. V5N 5T9 Tel:(604) 871-7000 Fax:(604) 871-7100
○ International Education Centre: 1080 Alberni Street, Vancouver, B.C. V6E 1A3 Tel:(604) 628-5900 Fax:(604) 628-5888

Vancouver Public Library presents

Paul Talbot

author of CLEAR THE CLUTTER & SIMPLIFY YOUR LIFE

Paths to Healing series

Spring Clean Your Clutter

tuesday march 6

7:30 p.m.
Alma VanDusen Room
Lower Level
Central Library
350 West Georgia St.
Admission is free
All are welcome

Vancouver Public Library
www.vpl.ca

Spring is here! It's time to do away with a winter's worth of clutter. Leap forward into Spring and set new goals with Paul Talbot. Join Paul for some practical pointers and advice. In the end, you will have plenty of time left over to stop and smell the cherry blossoms.

Paul Talbot, better know as the "No Clutter Guy", is an author, trainer, and simplicity coach. He is the creator of the *Clutter Series*.

Paul's website: www.dialaspeaker.com

For more information about VPL events, call the Events Line 604-331-3602 or go to www.vpl.ca

2004 Workshops with Paul Talbot

2004 WORKSHOPS WITH PAUL TALBOT

"Clear Your Clutter"
with Paul Talbot

It's 2004 and Time to

Sunday, **April 18, 2004** or
Sunday, **June 6, 2004**
10am to 4pm

If papers are piling high, closets filled with clothing of the last 20 years or more, too many "junk" drawers, magazines and books waiting to be read, bedrooms look like "warehouses", feel life is too cluttered then invest in one day with Paul Talbot. Paul is creator/founder of the Clutter Series and co-founder of End the Clutter International.

WHAT YOU WILL LEARN...
• How to sort and purge
• Design an Action Plan for your Clutter
• Identify areas that need immediate attention
• Where to Start Gathering the tools and resources and ways to simplify your life

"Clutter" can be physical, emotional, sentimental and mental. Discover new ways of "managing" your clutter.

Topics include:
• Household • Lifestyle • Finances • Job/Career
• Health • Personal Relationships • Core Simplicity

Workbook available at a special rate.

ASK ABOUT OUR MONTHLY DE-CLUTTER SUCCESS TEAMS!
Checkout our website at
www.endtheclutter.org

REGISTRATION DETAILS
•All registration fees include materials and coffee/lunch
•All workshops will be held at: **Rosedale on Robson Suite Hotel**
838 Hamilton Street, Vancouver, BC
(Check lobby board for Room)
•Parking Available

Paul Talbot has spoken in England, the United States and Canada. He was a key speaker at the 2002 Paul Toastmasters Conference (see reference letter on his website). He has appeared on Shaw TV, Global, CityTV, Urban Rush, Breakfast TV, CBC Radio up in the Globe & Mail, Family Circle, Vancouver Sun, The Courier, The Georgia Straight and other publications. He speaks four times a year at the Vancouver Public Library as part of the Healing Paths Series.

Seeking a speaker for that special event or LUNCH & LEARN? Need info on our workshops, consulting, coaching or Monthly De-Clutter Success Teams or Annual CLUTTER Reunion? Call 604 684 5059.

paul Talbot
No "Clutter Guy"

SPEAK AND EARN MONEY

Sunday, **June 13, 2004**
10am to 4pm

Spend a day with Paul Talbot - international speaker/trainer, published author, creator/founder of the "CLUTTER" Series, and co-founder of End the Clutter International.

DO YOU WANT TO....
Turn your skills, knowledge, experiences and passion into TOP DOLLARS?

Start your speaking career part-time and still keep your "other" job?

Share the life you LOVE but are afraid to take the risk?

WHAT YOU WILL LEARN...
• How to Choose a Topic
• Where to Start
• Free or Fee
• Ways to Market and Promote
• Free Coverage
• Sponsors
• Setting Fees (too high or low?)
• Creating an Image
• Brochure, Bio & Business Card
• Materials/Resources
• and more...

Simple & Forgotten Things©

Sunday, **June 27, 2004**
10am to 4pm

A one-day workshop on bringing **VOLUNTARY SIMPLICITY into your life.**

"You will find yourself again in the simple and forgotten things."
-CG Jung

This workshop introduces the subject of voluntary simplicity as an outward simple but inwardly rich way of life as an alternative to addictive consumerism and social inequality.

We will participate in a variety of exercises, reflections and simulation games that helps us identify the meaning our lives are striving to actualize, how we are currently deploying our time and energy and areas where we may decide to make new life choices.

We will also explore the values of simple living to the adventure of spiritual growth.

Please sign me up for:
(Tick box for each workshop you wish to be a part of)
☐ It's 2004 and Time to "Clear Your Clutter" with Paul Talbot - $85 per person
☐ Speak and Earn Money - $95 per person
☐ Simple & Forgotten Things - $95 per person

Name: _____

Address: _____

Postal Code: _____ Phone Number: _____

Email Address: _____

Checkout our website at
www.dialaspeaker.com
For more information phone 604 684 5059

Enclose cheque or money order payable to:
L. P. P. Talbot
with this form and mail to
PO Box 404 - 1196 Davie St.
Vancouver, BC, V6E 1N2

-113-

Services Offered by Paul Talbot

Paul Talbot, creator, founder and trainer of the "Clutter" series, is an international speaker, CLUTTER therapist, Simplicity Coach and published author. He is available for:

- Lunch & Learn
- After Dinner Talks
- Professional Day
- Employee Pick-Me-Up
- Special Events
- Conferences

His Talks, Speeches, Workshops, Seminars include:

<u>CLUTTER Series</u>:

- "I really, <u>Really</u>, **<u>REALLY</u>** want to clear my Clutter and get Organized!©"

- "Clear the Clutter & Simplify Your Life©"

- "Clear the Clutter for Senior©" (this he conducts through many Senior Centres & non-profit groups)

- "How to be a full/part-time Clutter Organizer©"

- "Simple and Forgotten Thing – Voluntary Simplicity©"

- One hour and up Clutter topics:

    - Clear Your Desk Clutter
    - Cluttered Small Spaces
    - Procrastinator's Workshop
    - Conquer Your Clutter
    - Cluttered Papers 101
    - Household Clutter
    - Cluttered Closets
    - Cluttered Relationships
    - How to Organize Your Cluttered Photo's
    - Will Your Christmas be Cluttered)? (November / December only)

Other Topics Include:

- "L.O.V.E. Living Our Values Everyday©"

- "How to Facilitate with Facts, Feelings and Fun©"

- "Don't Count the Candles – It's Just a Number!©"

- "Is self-employment an option for you?©"

- "Relationship building through Mind Mapping©"

- "Putting Fun and Laughter back into your Life©"

- "How to Earn Money as a Speaker©"

- Feeling Fabulous At Any Age

For complete bio and details on other services (including this self-published book by Paul

Talbot), please refer to our website. If you are seeking a speaker/trainer with a difference, remember "PAUL TALBOT" the no-clutter guy.

If you are interested in becoming a facilitator of any of the "Clutter" series, please contact us.

Paul is available as your own Personal Clutter Re-Organizer or, if you feel that your life is in a mess call him about his services as:

The Simplicity Coach

As "Clear the Clutter" coach, the focus is on the client's current life, desires, plans, goals, vision and future.
Coaching is about focussing on the whole person. Let him guide you towards finding balance, love and joy in your life.

This is our purpose: *to make as meaningful as possible the life that has been bestowed upon us, ...to live is such a way that we may be proud of ourselves, to act in such a way that some part of us lives on.*

Oswald Spengler, German Philosopher

To reach Paul in Canada:	Paul Talbot "No-Clutter Guy" Creator/Founder PO Box 404 1195 Davie Street Vancouver, BC V6E IN2 Website: www.dialaspeaker.com Email: admin@dialaspeaker.com

Speakers, Meeting Planners, Bureaus, Agents & Consultants
SHARING IDEAS

Oct/Nov   *NEWS MAGAZINE*

SUBSCRIBE NOW!

2 year subscription includes:

- Directory of over 500 Speakers Bureaus & Agencies from 19 countries

- "How to be Booked by Speakers Bureaus" – audio album

2 Years @ $95.00 + $5 ship./hand. 1st package only
Canada / Mexico, $124
Other Countries, $175

ALL ORDERS IN US FUNDS
Check Enclosed or Charge my...

Visa ☐   MasterCard ☐   American Exp. ☐   Discover ☐

Card #

Expiry date
Signature
Name
Address
City
Prov. / State
Postal code/ZIP
Phone
Fax / Cell

Mail to: Royal Publishing
PO Box 398
Glendora, CA 91740 USA
Tel: 626-335-8069 Fax: 626-335-6127
www.SpeakAndGrowRich.com

FAMOUS QUOTES

"Since this is my only life, I just want to live forever. The only way I can accomplish that is to make a difference in the lives of others."
– Gina Ginsberg Riggs
Executive Director
Gifted Child Society Inc.
New Jersey

"You just never know what's around the corner!"
– Joan Sutterland
Opera Singer
New York

"When Opportunity knocks on your door, accept it."
– Jane Wyatt
Actress
California

"Be Free!"
– Eddie Murphy
Actor
California

"When Kindness or Understanding happens unexpectedly, there is no greater delight."
– William Bolcom
Musician, Composer, Educator
University of Michigan
School of Music

ISBN 142513949-3